EIBHLÍN MILNER

A NATIVITY PLAY FOR ALL PRIMARY SCHOOL CHILDREN

(with production notes and stage directions)

STEP-BY-STEP DRAMA

First published 1998 by
Veritas Publications
7-8 Lower Abbey Street
Dublin 1

ISBN 1 85390 399 X

Cover design by Colette Dower
Cover illustration by Bill Bolger
Printed in the Republic of Ireland by Pace Print Ltd, Dublin

CONTENTS

FOREWORD

This nativity play has been written in such a way as to make its production as easy as possible for the teacher. A list of the entire cast, an outline of the drama itself, stage diagrams and easy-to-follow notes on direction and production are provided.

This drama can be adapted to suit any age-group, from four-year-olds to twelve-year-olds. It can take up to forty/forty-five minutes to perform, depending on how many children are involved and how many carols you choose to include. If you wish to confine your production to a biblical nativity play alone, The Gift *can be very easily adapted and the drama, if the secular sub-plot is excluded, would take about thirty minutes to perform. All options are discussed in detail within.*

The play is suitable for production in school or church, youth centre or parish hall. I hope that it provides much enjoyment and joy wherever it is performed. Perhaps, in its simplicity, it might succeed in reminding each of us to bring Christ into Christmas.

Nollaig shona dhaoibh go léir!

EIBHLÍN MILNER

CAST

Community Cast (10)

Deirdre	(leading lady)
Liam	(leading lad)
Mother	1
Father	1
Postman	1
Neighbours	3
Returning emigrants (American cousins)	3

The Spirit of Christmas (3)

Spirit 1	1
Spirit 2	1
Spirit 3	1

Nativity Cast (14)

Mary	1
Joseph	1
Angel Gabriel	1
Donkey	1
Innkeeper	1
Shepherds	3
Angels	3
Kings	3

Narrators (2)

Narrator 1	(Simeon)
Narrator 2	(Anna)

The suggested cast, above, includes thirty children. However, this number can easily be increased or decreased to suit your particular needs. (See 'Making Choices', p. 41)

OUTLINE OF DRAMA

Scene 1: Ready for Christmas?
The opening scene reveals all the preparations that have been made for Christmas by Deirdre and Liam and their family and friends. However, three mysterious visitors suddenly arrive on the scene – the 'Spirit of Christmas'! They remind Deirdre and Liam of the real reason for all these celebrations. It's Jesus' birthday, yet no one seems to have remembered him.

Song 1:   'Winter Wonderland' (played on CD or tape)

Scene 2: A Visit to the East
The spirits use a time-machine to transport the children and their friends back in time. They visit the Holy Land in the year of Jesus' birth. Simeon and Anna narrate the nativity story. This scene includes the annuciation, the visitation and the journey to Bethlehem.

Instrumental 1:	Passage through Time
Instrumental 2:	'The Little Drummer Boy'
Song 2:	'The Little Drummer Boy'
Song 3:	'Song for Mary'
Song 4:	'Little Donkey'

Scene 3: The Little Town of Bethlehem
Mary and Joseph, refused shelter in an inn, seek refuge in a nearby stable.

Scene 4: The Gift
In this scene we meet the shepherds, the angels and the wise kings. A bright star leads them to the stable in Bethlehem, the birthplace of the infant Jesus.

Instrumental 3:	'Away in a Manger'
Song 5:	'Away in a Manger'
Song 6:	'Gloria in excelsis Deo'

Scene 5: Happy Birthday, Jesus
In this final scene Mary, Joseph and the Infant take their places front stage. Angels, shepherds and kings surround them. A procession of light follows as Deirdre and Liam arrive to visit the manger. All on stage wish Jesus a happy birthday. 'Silent Night' is sung. Deirdre and Liam thank the spirits for helping them to remember the real meaning of Christmas. The drama ends with 'Mary's Boy Child'.

Instrumental 4:	Arrival of the Christ-child (Procession of Light)
Song 7:	'Silent Night'/'Oíche Ciúin'
Song 8:	'Mary's Boy Child'

Note: Optional ending of drama on completion of Song 7, 'Silent Night'/'Oíche Chiúin'.

STAGE SET-UP

Note the positions of the characters on stage as Scene 1 begins. There are seven actors on stage, seven actors side stage, right and left, and seventeen actors (biblical characters) back stage.

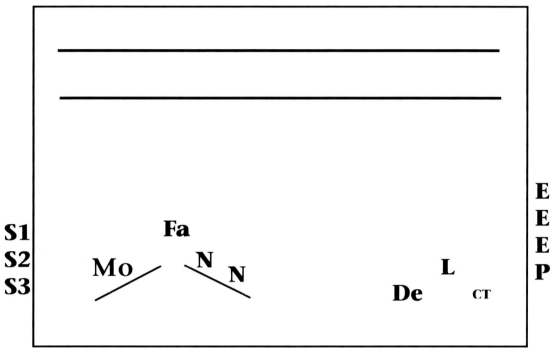

A= Angel (*A=Angel Gabriel)	S1, S2, S3= Spirit of Christmas
S= Shepherd	N= Neighbour
K= King	E= Emigrant
M= Mary	P= Postman
J= Joseph	Mo= Mother
N1= Simeon	Fa= Father
N2= Anna	De= Deirdre
Do= Donkey	L= Liam
I= Innkeeper	CT= *Christmas Tree*
EL= Elizabeth	

Note also the abbreviations used to represent each character on stage. These abbreviations will be used throughout the detailed staging notes.

Drama Script

SCENE 1

READY FOR CHRISTMAS?

Note: The script is given here with minimal production notes and staging instructions. Once the children are familiar with their lines and you are ready to move on to the business of stage set-ups etc, you could work from the version on pp. 24-40, which includes comprehensive staging and production notes.

Song 1: *Winter Wonderland* (background music, on CD or tape)

Mimed opening scenes

Mother and three neighbours chat, drink tea and share some Christmas baking delights.

Father stands by the music-centre, browsing through some Christmas records, as if he has just put 'Winter Wonderland' on to play.

Deirdre and Liam decorate the tree, smiling and laughing excitedly as they show decorations to each other, while their parents tidy the presents that lie underneath the tree.

After some time Father opens the door to the postman and welcomes him inside to share a cuppa. The postman delivers some colourful cards and nicely wrapped parcels. Father slips him a Christmas 'thank you' in an envelope and the postman gladly accepts the cash donation with a wink!

Shortly afterwards, Mother answers the door and greets her American cousins with hugs and kisses. They join the neighbours for a welcome cuppa while Deirdre and Liam happily accept American gifts and place them under the tree.

As Song 1 ends, Father leads the postman and neighbours to the front door (i.e. side-stage left) and all wave goodbye. Then Father and Mother lead the visiting emigrants 'upstairs' (i.e. side-stage right) to settle them into their guest rooms, leaving Deirdre and Liam alone in the sitting-room.

As neighbours, parents and guests leave the sitting-room, Liam goes to the music-centre and lowers the volume of the music, slowly, until it is inaudible. (You don't want the music to drown out the actors' voices, but you also need to make sure that the transition from lively music to chat is made smoothly and not too harshly.)

Deirdre	I love Christmas! All that lovely food, mmm... and the presents... *(Moving towards the Christmas tree and picking up the presents one at a time.)* This one's for Mam... this one's for Dad... and this one is for our little baby sister...
All	Aah...
	A loud knock on the door is heard.
Liam	What's that? *(The knocking continues.)* Who is it? I know there's SOMEBODY there.
	Enter three mysterious-looking figures. Deirdre and Liam jump back and clutch each other momentarily, in fright.
Deirdre and Liam	*(in a shocked and frightened tone)* GHOSTS!
Spirits	*(laughing)* We're not ghosts!

Deirdre	Well, you certainly look like ghosts.
Spirits	(*doing a twirl and taking a bow*) We're the Spirit of Christmas!
Liam	(*looking rather puzzled*) The Spirit of Christmas?
Spirit 1	(*the serious spirit, who has all his work detailed in a large red notebook*) Yes, and we're VERY busy at the moment... (*carefully examining his notebook*).
Spirit 2	(*having a little stretch.*) That's why we're so tired...
Spirit 3	(*yawning*) So EXHAUSTED... (*bending low and rubbing his back as if he is in great pain and can walk no further*) I simply MUST take a seat.
Deirdre	Come, sit down over here. (*Brings Spirit 3 over to a comfy armchair where he reclines in a very relaxed position!*)
Liam	Now, tell us, what are you doing here?
Spirit 1	We've come to bring the REAL Spirit of Christmas to this home!
Liam:	(*In a confused and insulted tone*) The REAL spirit of Christmas? What do you mean? We have everything... the tree, the cards, the decorations...
Deirdre	The presents, the turkey... EVERYTHING! What more could there be?
Spirit 2	(*in a disappointed tone*) They've forgotten, haven't they?
Liam:	(*getting angrier*) Forgotten WHAT?
Spirit 2	Shall we tell them?
Deirdre and Liam	(*impatiently*) Tell us, tell us!
Spirit 3	You've forgotten WHY everybody is celebrating...
Deirdre	(*arrogantly*) Oh no we haven't... it's Christmas!
Spirit 1	Yes, it's Christmas, it's Jesus' birthday.
Spirit 3	Where's HIS present?
Deirdre	(*a little taken aback, she goes to the tree in search of Jesus' birthday present, but finds nothing*) I suppose we have forgotten...
Spirit 2	(*Putting his arm around Deirdre to console her*) Don't be troubled, lots of people forget amid all this rush and chaos.
Spirit 1	That's why we drop in, to help bring the real Spirit of Christmas to live in every home.
Liam	And how, exactly, are you going to manage that?
Spirit 1	We're going to take you on a trip, back in time, a trip to the Holy Land, to the place of Jesus' birth (*taking out what looks like a mini-computer*).
All	(*in amazement*) Wow!
Spirit 3	Try to get it right this time! Last time he used this time-machine I ended up with Daniel, in the Lion's den. . . and guess who was on the menu?

Spirit 2   Hey there, no need to get so edgy.

Spirit 3:   Hold on to your hats, folks, we're on our way…

INSTRUMENTAL 1   ***Passage through time*** (see note p. 27)

SCENE 2

A VISIT TO THE EAST

Spirit 1   Simeon, Anna! It's so good to see you. *(Simeon and Anna nod graciously)*

Liam   *(anxiously)* Where are we? Who are these strangers?

Deirdre   I'm scared!

Spirit 3   Don't start crying ... please don't cry. *(Aside to the audience)* I hate it when they cry!

Spirit 2 walks towards Deirdre and Liam and gives them a reassuring squeeze on the arm.

Spirit 2   Now, now, there's no need to worry. These are our Eastern friends. They're very good storytellers and they are going to help us to tell the story of Jesus' birthday.

INSTRUMENTAL 2   ***The Little Drummer Boy***

SONG 2   ***The Little Drummer Boy*** **(if sung)**

Come, they told me, parum pum pum pum,
A newborn king to see parum pum pum pum,
Our finest gifts we bring, parum pum pum pum,
To lay before the king, parum pum pum pum,
Rum pum pum pum, rum pum pum pum,
So to honour him, parum pum pum pum,
When we come.

Baby Jesus......
I am a poor boy too......
I have no gift to bring......
That's fit to give our king......
Shall I play for you......
On my drum?

Mary nodded......
The ox and lamb kept time......
I played my drum for him......
I played my best for him......
Then he smiled at me......
Me and my drum.

Narrator 1   Mary was working at home one day, when suddenly she heard an angel say...

Gabriel   Mary, will you be the mother of God?

All   Yes, replied Mary, with a simple nod.

SONG 3   ***Song for Mary***

Mary, will you take this baby boy?
Mary, will you take this baby boy?
Will you fill the world with love and joy?
Will you take this baby boy?
Mary, will you go to the little town?

Mary, will you go to the little town?
Will you find a manger to lay him down?
Will you go to the little town?

Mary, will you tell him that we love him so?
Mary, will you tell him that we love him so?
Will you tell him we would like to show
That we love him, love him so.

All

Mary made a good choice,
God was really pleased!
She would bear a son
Who would care for all our needs.

Narrator 2

She went to visit her cousin,
Elizabeth was her name.
She too had news of a baby boy,
John, a son who would bring great joy.

All

Joseph soon heard the wonderful news,
The news of a new baby boy.
Joseph hugged Mary and gave her his help
As his heart filled with peace, love and joy.

Narrator 1

A census was held in a city afar –
Bethlehem, city of David.
They travelled by donkey, a very long way,
Guided only by light of a star.

All

They loaded the donkey and set off on the road,
Mary, with Joseph at her side.
They knew they would be weary,
They knew they would be weak,
With so many miles to ride.

SONG **4**

Little Donkey

Little donkey, little donkey, on the dusty road.
Gotta keep on plodding onwards, with your precious load.
Been a long time, little donkey, through the winter nights.
Don't give up now, little donkey, Bethlehem's in sight.

Ring out those bells tonight! Bethlehem! Bethlehem!
Follow that star tonight! Bethlehem! Bethlehem!
Little donkey, little donkey, had a heavy day.
Little donkey, carry Mary safely on her way.

Scene 3

The little town of Bethlehem

Mary	Joseph, look at all the crowds!
All	Said Mary, as they reached the town.
Joseph	Will we ever find a place to stay?
All	Thought Joseph, with a fearful frown.

Joseph and Mary walk towards the inn, to ask for help.

Narrator 2	Joseph knocked upon a door. The innkeeper said:
Innkeeper	No! The inn is full. . . you can't come in! To the stables you will have to go!
Narrator 1	Joseph then took Mary's hand. Together they headed away In search of a stable, dark and cold, For a baby who would save the world.
Instrumental 3	**Away in a manger**
Song 5	***Away in a manger***

Away in a manger, no crib for a bed.
The little Lord Jesus laid down his sweet head.
The stars in the bright sky looked down where he lay,
The little Lord Jesus, asleep on the hay.
The cattle are lowing, the baby awakes,
But little Lord Jesus, no crying he makes.
I love you Lord Jesus, look down from the sky
And stay by my bedside until morning is nigh.
Be near me Lord Jesus, I ask you to stay
Close by me forever and love me, I pray.
Bless all the dear children in your loving care
And fit us for heaven to live with you there.

SCENE 4

THE GIFT

As 'Away in a Manger' ends, three shepherds walk front stage. One stands, gazing at the sky, staff in hand. Another curls up on the ground, sleeping. A third kneels on one knee, watching, listening, guarding. The angels get ready to 'appear'.

Narrator 2

On a hillside shepherds were minding their sheep,
Watching and guarding all night.
One heard music, a beautiful air.
He jumped! Then he ran in fright.

The shepherd who was on bended knee jumps up in fright and runs towards his friends.

Shepherd

Listen! Such music I've not heard before.
Look at the angels! What could be in store?

All

The angels gave the shepherds the news of such great joy.
A Saviour had been born! A Saviour...Christ the Lord!

Narrator 1

The shepherds set off in great joy and glee
Listening to the angels sing of praise and glory.

SONG 6

Gloria in Excelsis Deo

Glo......ria! In excelsis Deo.
Glo......ria! In excelsis Deo.

As Song 6, 'Gloria in Excelsis Deo', finishes, the angels and shepherds leave the stage. Three kings then come forward and stand front stage.

Narrator 1

Away in the east three kings were confused
For the stars were quite different that night.
Their books could not tell them, their books they did fail
To reveal the dear Saviour's birth.

King 1

Look at that star... Oh what can it mean?

All

The first king questioned it so.
The second king smiled as the third, he did say...

King 3

We will follow that star, come what may!

Narrators 1 and 2

So they gathered their gifts and followed that star
With frankincense, gold and myrrh.

All

Not knowing the joy that soon lay in store, when each one
would tremble and quiver...

The kings leave the stage, excitedly, in search of the special child.

20

SCENE 5

HAPPY BIRTHDAY JESUS!

INSTRUMENTAL 4   *Arrival of the Christ-child* (see notes p. 37)

As Instrumental 4 continues, the lights on stage are dimmed. Slowly, Mary and Joseph come on to the stage, holding the infant. They take their tableau positions.

All	For there in the manger the little boy lay Asleep, fast asleep on the soft golden hay.

As the instrumental music continues, one by one the visitors come to the manger. First the kings, then the shepherds and finally the angels. They take their positions in the tableau...some kneeling, some standing, heads bowed in adoration.

PROCESSION OF LIGHT *(Optional)*

As the manger tableau is completed, Deirdre and Liam step backstage momentarily and return with two lighted candles. They walk, solemnly, to take their places front stage. As the instrumental fades, they lift the candles slowly as everyone on stage wishes Jesus a very happy birthday.

All:	HAPPY BIRTHDAY, JESUS!
SONG 7	***Silent Night***

> Silent Night, Holy Night,
> All is calm, all is bright.
> Round yon Virgin, Mother and Child,
> Holy Infant so tender and mild.
> Sleep in heavenly peace,
> Sleep in heavenly peace.
>
> Oíche chiúin, oíche Mhic Dé,
> Cách na suan, dís araon,
> Dís is dílse faire le spéir,
> Naíon beag gnaoigheal ceananntais caomh,
> Críost 'na chodladh go séimh,
> Críost 'na chodladh go séimh.

Spirit 1	I'm afraid our journey is almost over. Soon we'll be returning you back home again.
Deirdre	How can we ever thank you?
Spirit 3	I suppose some light refreshments would be out of the question?
Spirit 1	Yes they would! We can't have you gurgling your way forward to the twentieth century.
Liam	We'll never forget this amazing adventure, and of course now we can't EVER forget the real Spirit of Christmas.
Spirit 3	Looks like we've done a good job then! Now let's see where is our next assignment?
Spirit 1	Bedrock, California.
Spirit 3	Yabadabadoo!

21

Liam   Before you start pushing any of those buttons *(pointing to the computer)* we'd really like to make you a promise...

Spirit 2   A promise?

All candle-bearers Yes! We'd like to promise that at Christmastime,
We'll STOP! And think of him,
We'll give a little time to the one who matters most –
Jesus, our Lord and our King.

Deirdre and Liam shake hands with the spirits and there are some emotional hugs and goodbyes as all join in the finale.

SONG 8/FINALE   ***Mary's Boy Child***

A long time ago in Bethlehem so the Holy Bible says,
Mary's boy child, Jesus Christ, was born on Christmas Day.

Chorus:
Hark now hear the angels sing, 'A new king born today',
And man will live for ever more because of Christmas Day.
Trumpets sound and angels sing, listen to what they say...
That man will live for ever more because of Christmas Day.

While shepherds watch their flocks by night,
They see a bright new shining star.
They hear a choir sing a song, the music seems to come from afar.
Now Joseph and his wife Mary come to Bethlehem that night.
They find no place to lay the child, not a single room in sight.

Chorus

By and by they find a little nook in a stable so forlorn,
And in a manger cold and dark Mary's little boy was born.

Chorus

Drama Script with Production Notes and Stage Diagrams

SCENE 1

READY FOR CHRISTMAS?

SONG 1   *Winter Wonderland*

The song which fills the air as the curtains open is 'Winter Wonderland'. This song is played on record, tape or CD to create the Christmas atmosphere. (There is no need to teach this song to the children, but if you would prefer them to sing it or to sing along with the record, that's fine also). The actors on stage then mime the opening scenes to the strains of 'Winter Wonderland'.

* If 'Winter Wonderland' on its own is too short to accommodate all the first mimed scenes you can always continue with any other Christmas song on your CD or tape. It doesn't matter which Christmas song is playing as the mimed scenes end, as Liam will be lowering the volume of the music to begin his chat with Deirdre in the first spoken scene of the play. The opening song is designed to create the scene of secular Christmas festivities, so you can use any secular Christmas songs (as opposed to religious Christmas carols).

Stage set-up

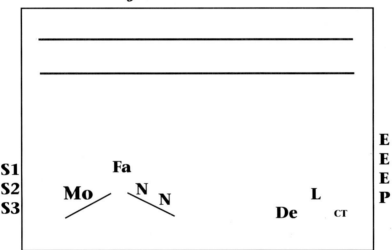

Mimed opening scenes

Mother and three neighbours chat, drink tea and share some Christmas baking delights.

Father stands by the music-centre, browsing through some Christmas records, as if he has just put 'Winter Wonderland' on to play.

Deirdre and Liam decorate the tree, smiling and laughing excitedly as they show decorations to each other, while their parents tidy the presents that lie underneath the tree.

After some time Father opens the door to the postman and welcomes him inside to share a cuppa. The postman delivers some colourful cards and nicely wrapped parcels. Father slips him a Christmas 'thank you' in an envelope and the postman gladly accepts the cash donation with a wink!

Shortly afterwards, Mother answers the door and greets her American cousins with hugs and kisses. They join the neighbours for a welcome cuppa while Deirdre and Liam happily accept American gifts and place them under the tree.

As Song 1 ends Father leads the postman and neighbours to the front door (i.e. side-stage left) and all wave goodbye. Then Father and Mother lead the visiting emigrants 'upstairs' (i.e. side-stage right), to settle them into their guest rooms, leaving Deirdre and Liam alone in the sitting-room.

As neighbours, parents and guests leave the sitting-room, Liam goes to the music-centre and lowers the volume, slowly, until it is inaudible. (You don't want the music to drown out the actors' voices, but you also need to make sure that the transition from lively music to chat is made smoothly and not too harshly.)

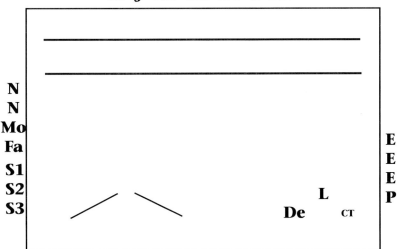

Deirdre   I love Christmas! All that lovely food, mmm... and the presents... *(Moving towards the Christmas tree and picking up the presents one at a time.)* This one's for Mam...this one's for Dad...and this one is for our little baby sister...

All   Aah...

A loud knock on the door is heard...

Liam: What's that? *(The knocking continues...)* Who is it? I know there's SOMEBODY there.

Enter three mysterious-looking figures. Deirdre and Liam jump back and clutch each other, momentarily, in fright.

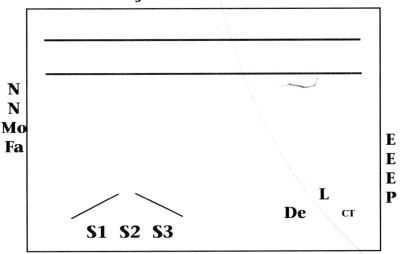

Deirdre and Liam *(in a shocked and frightened tone)* GHOSTS!

Spirits   *(laughing)* We're not ghosts!

Deirdre   Well, you certainly look like ghosts.

Spirits	*(Doing a twirl and taking a bow)* We're the Spirit of Christmas!
Liam	*(Looking rather puzzled.)* The Spirit of Christmas?
Spirit 1	*(The serious spirit, who has all his work detailed in a large red notebook)* Yes, and we're VERY busy at the moment... *(carefully examining his notebook)*
Spirit 2	*(Having a little stretch.)* That's why we're so tired...
Spirit 3	*(Yawning)* So EXHAUSTED... *(bending low and rubbing his back as if he is in great pain and can walk no further)* I simply MUST take a seat.
Deirdre	Come, sit down over here... *(brings Spirit 3 over to a comfy armchair where he reclines in a very relaxed position!)*

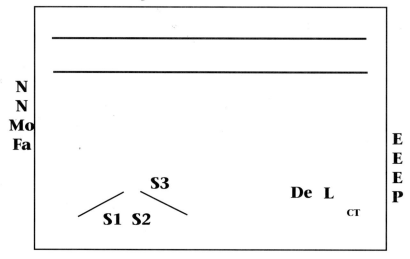

Liam	Now, tell us, what are you doing here?
Spirit 1	We've come to bring the REAL Spirit of Christmas to this home!
Liam	*(in a confused and insulted tone)* The REAL spirit of Christmas? What do you mean? We have everything. . . the tree, the cards, the decorations. . .
Deirdre	The presents, the turkey. . . EVERYTHING! What more could there be?
Spirit 2	*(in a disappointed tone)* They've forgotten, haven't they?
Liam	*(getting angrier)* Forgotten WHAT?
Spirit 2	Shall we tell them?
Deirdre and Liam	*(impatiently)* Tell us, tell us!
Spirit 3	You've forgotten WHY everybody is celebrating . . .
Deirdre	*(arrogantly)* Oh no we haven't. . . it's Christmas!
Spirit 1	Yes, it's Christ-mas, it's Jesus' birthday.
Spirit 3	Where's HIS present?
Deirdre	*(a little taken aback, she goes to the tree in search of Jesus' birthday present, but finds nothing)* I suppose we have forgotten. . .

Spirit 2	*(putting his arm around Deirdre to console her)* Don't be troubled, lots of people forget amid all this rush and chaos…
Spirit 1	That's why we drop in, to help bring the real Spirit of Christmas to life in every home.
Liam	And how, exactly, are you going to manage that?
Spirit 1	We're going to take you on a trip, back in time, a trip to the Holy Land, to the place of Jesus' birth… *(taking out what looks like a mini-computer)*
All	*(in amazement)* Wow!
Spirit 3	Try to get it right this time! Last time he used this time-machine I ended up with Daniel, in the Lion's den… and guess who was on the menu?
Spirit 2	Hey there, no need to get so edgy.
Spirit 3	Hold on to your hats, folks, we're on our way…

INSTRUMENTAL 1   ***Passage through time***

You can choose any piece of instrumental music you deem suitable for a magical journeying through time, e.g. a haunting piece of music from Enya or something as simple as 'The Little Drummer Boy', played instrumentally to introduce the biblical theme. The piece I find particularly suitable and effective is 'Eric's Theme', from the soundtrack of the film Chariots of Fire.

Spirit 1 presses the magic buttons of the time-machine and suddenly a haunting music fills the air. Lights flash on and off, on stage if possible. Deirdre and Liam remain centre-stage as the biblical characters take their new positions on stage as shown below. Note that the narrators are front stage and that the other 'secular' actors also return on stage at this time, somewhat inconspicuously, to help with the singing.

As Scene 1 ends, Spirit 1 walks across the stage to greet the narrators.

Scene 2

A Visit to the East

```
Mo  F *A A A A S S S K K K    E E
    ┌─────────────────────────────────
    │ N   M J        Do I EL     E P
  N └─────────────────────────────────



               De  L


                              S2 S3
      N1 N2 S1                     CT
```

Spirit 1   Simeon, Anna! It's so good to see you. *(Simeon and Anna nod graciously)*

Liam   *(anxiously)* Where are we? Who are these strangers?

Deirdre   I'm scared!

Spirit 3   Don't start crying... please don't cry. *(Aside to the audience)* I hate it when they cry!

Spirit 2 walks towards Deirdre and Liam and gives them a reassuring squeeze on the arm.

Spirit 2   Now, now, there's no need to worry. These are our Eastern friends. They're very good storytellers and they are going to help us to tell the story of Jesus' birthday.

```
Mo  F  A A A S S S K K K    E E
    ┌──────────────────────────────
    │ N  J   De L  Do I EL    E P
    └──────────────────────────────

                *A


                    M
      N1      N2
        Dr              S1 S2 S3
                                 CT
```

INSTRUMENTAL 2   *The Little Drummer Boy*
As the instrumental 'The Little Drummer Boy' is being played, Deirdre and Liam skip back happily, as Spirits 1 and 2 return to their positions front stage. Mary and the Angel Gabriel take their positions front stage. Make sure they take their time – there is no need for anyone to rush around the stage!

If you wish to sing a verse or two of 'The little Drummer Boy' then go ahead and do so. One of the 'neighbours' who appeared earlier could return on stage during the 'Passage through Time', at the same time as the little drummer boy/and stand front stage beside the narrators as the song is being sung. Note the abbreviation **Dr for the Drummer Boy.*

SONG 2	***The Little Drummer Boy (if sung)***

Come, they told me, parum pum pum pum,
A newborn king to see parum pum pum pum,
Our finest gifts we bring, parum pum pum pum,
To lay before the king, parum pum pum pum,
Rum pum pum pum, rum pum pum pum,
So to honour him, parum pum pum pum,
When we come.

Baby Jesus......
I am a poor boy too......
I have no gift to bring......
That's fit to give our king......
Shall I play for you......
On my drum?

Mary nodded......
The ox and lamb kept time......
I played my drum for him......
I played my best for him......
Then he smiled at me......
Me and my drum.

The Drummer Boy returns to his place at the back of the stage as the song ends, marching in time with the music. He will be referred to as **N** *once more throughout the stage diagrams.*

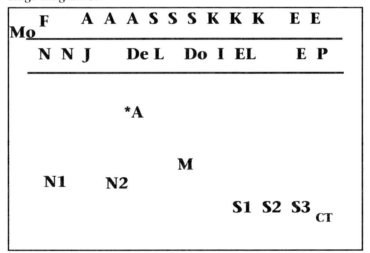

Narrator 1	Mary was working at home one day, When suddenly she heard an angel say...
Gabriel	Mary, will you be the mother of God?
All	Yes, replied Mary, with a simple nod.
SONG 3	***Song for Mary***

Mary, will you take this baby boy?
Mary, will you take this baby boy?
Will you fill the world with love and joy?
Will you take this baby boy?

Mary, will you go to the little town?
Mary, will you go to the little town?
Will you find a manger to lay him down?
Will you go to the little town?

Mary, will you tell him that we love him so?
Mary, will you tell him that we love him so?
Will you tell him we would like to show
That we love him love him so......

All

Mary made a good choice,
God was really pleased!
She would bear a son
Who would care for all our needs.

The angel Gabriel returns to his place, backstage. Elizabeth takes her place on stage. Slowly,
Mary walks to her and they embrace and 'chat' as if telling each other their exciting news.

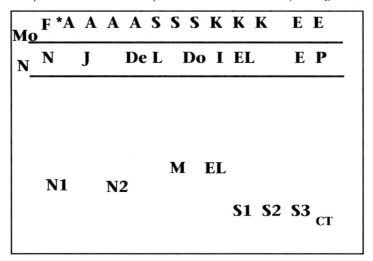

Narrator 2

She went to visit her cousin,
Elizabeth was her name.
She too had news of a baby boy,
John, a son who would bring great joy.

Mary waves goodbye to her cousin and walks towards front stage. Elizabeth returns to
her place. Joseph rushes forward, as if he has just heard the news. At first he seems
confused and questioning, but as Mary explains all, he hugs her and is fully supportive.

```
Mo  F *A  A  A  A  S  S  S  K  K  K    E  E
N    N        De L   Do  I  EL       E  P



              J   M



   N1     N2              S1 S2 S3
                                   CT
```

All

Joseph soon heard the wonderful news,
The news of a new baby boy.
Joseph hugged Mary and gave her his help
As his heart filled with peace, love and joy.

Narrator 1

A census was held in a city afar
Bethlehem, city of David.

They travelled by donkey, a very long way,
Guided only by light of a star.

The donkey takes his place in front of Mary and Joseph

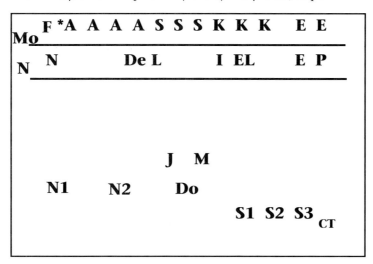

All   They loaded the donkey and set off on the road,
Mary, with Joseph at her side.
They knew they would be weary,
They knew they would be weak,
With so many miles to ride...

SONG 4   ***Little Donkey***

Little donkey, little donkey, on the dusty road.
Gotta keep on plodding onwards, with your precious load.
Been a long time, little donkey, through the winter nights.
Don't give up now, little donkey, Bethlehem's in sight.

Ring out those bells tonight! Bethlehem! Bethlehem!
Follow that star tonight! Bethlehem! Bethlehem!
Little donkey, little donkey, had a heavy day.
Little donkey, carry Mary safely on her way.

As 'Little Donkey' is being sung, Mary and Joseph – and the donkey! –travel around the stage, in a circle, as if journeying towards Bethlehem. If the donkey is musical, he could play some bells during the chorus of the carol – 'Ring out those bells tonight', etc!

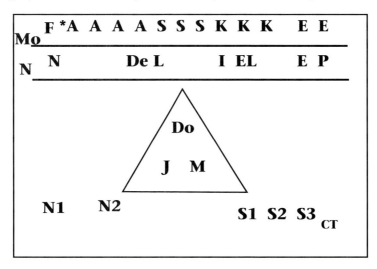

31

Towards the end of the carol, having completed a circle of the stage, Joseph, Mary and the donkey stand front stage once more.

```
Mo  F *A A A A S S S K K K   E E
N    N        De L      I EL    E P



                  J  M
    N1      N2      Do
                      S1 S2 S3 CT
```

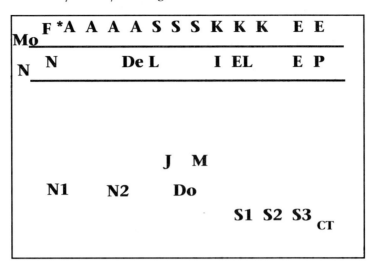

As the carol finishes, the donkey heads back to his place. The innkeeper takes his place on stage. If you want to enlarge the inn scene you can include some people in the inn, sitting at tables or just standing around gossiping about these 'strangers'. Scene 3 is very simple with just one character, namely the innkeeper. He could come to the 'door', wearing an apron and carrying an urn of wine in his hand. Mary and Joseph look front stage at 'the crowds', i.e. the audience.

SCENE 3

THE LITTLE TOWN OF BETHLEHEM

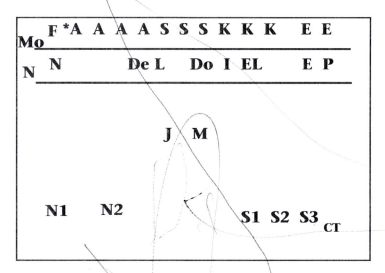

Mary appears frightened as she points out all the crowds. Joseph is also concerned.

Mary   Joseph, look at all the crowds!

All   Said Mary, as they reached the town.

Joseph   Will we ever find a place to stay?

All   Thought Joseph, with a fearful frown.

Joseph and Mary walk towards the inn, to ask for help.

Narrator 2   Joseph knocked upon a door.
The innkeeper said:

Innkeeper   No! The inn is full...you can't come in!
To the stables you will have to go!

Joseph puts his arm around Mary, to console her, as hand in hand they then turn around and walk off the stage, to the stables.

Narrator 1   Joseph then took Mary's hand.
Together they headed away
In search of a stable, dark and cold,
For a baby who would save the world.

33

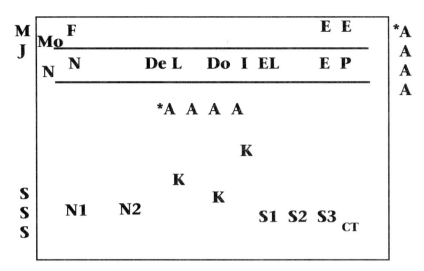

King 1	Look at that star...oh, what can it mean?
All:	The first king questioned it so. The second king smiled as the third, he did say...
King 3	We will follow that star, come what may!
Narrators 1 and 2	So they gathered their gifts and followed that star With frankincense, gold and myrrh.
All	Not knowing the joy that soon lay in store, when each one would tremble and quiver.

The kings leave the stage excitedly, in search of the special child.

SCENE 5

HAPPY BIRTHDAY JESUS!

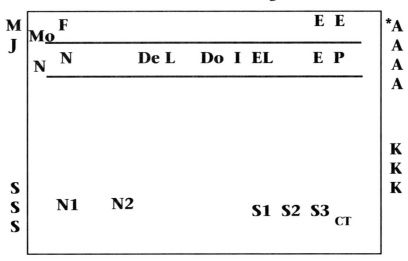

INSTRUMENTAL 4   *Arrival of the Christ-child*

Choose any piece of poignant music to herald the birth of Jesus. You could use a rendition of 'Ave Maria' played on tape or you might like the children to play 'Silent Night' instrumentally. A piece that I feel captures the essence of this moment is 'Abraham's Theme' from the soundtrack of the film Chariots of Fire. *The opening bars of music suit the procession of Mary and Joseph to front stage very well. Then, a few bars into the piece the music increases in volume and there is a stirring musical moment, which suits the 'lifting' of the tiny child by Mary and Joseph as they hold the infant aloft for all to see.*

(a) As Instrumental 4 begins, the children at the back of the stage can tidy up their positions, getting ready for the final tableau to take its place front stage.

(b) As Instrumental 4 continues, the lights on stage are dimmed. Slowly, Mary and Joseph come onto the stage, holding the infant.

(c) Mary and Joseph walk, from the back entrance of the stage, forward to front stage to take their tableau positions.

ALL   For there in the manger the little boy lay
                     Asleep, fast asleep on the soft golden hay.

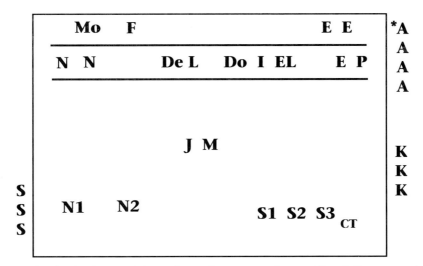

As the instrumental music continues, one by one the visitors come to the manger. First the kings, then the shepherds and finally the angels. They take their positions in the tableau...some kneeling, some standing, heads bowed in adoration.

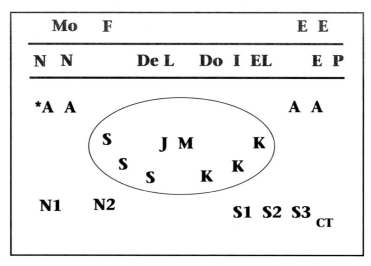

Procession of Light (Optional)

As the manger tableau is completed, Deirdre and Liam step backstage momentarily and return with two lighted candles. They walk, solemnly, to take their places front stage. As the instrumental fades, they lift the candles slowly as everyone on stage wishes Jesus a very happy birthday.

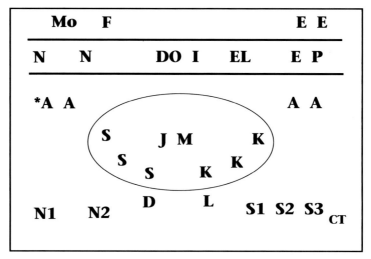

All   HAPPY BIRTHDAY JESUS!

A verse or two of 'Silent Night' is sung in English or Irish, or alternatively a verse in either language – whatever suits.

Song 7   *Silent Night*

Silent Night, Holy Night,
All is calm, all is bright.
Round yon Virgin, Mother and Child,
Holy Infant so tender and mild.
Sleep in heavenly peace,
Sleep in heavenly peace.

Oíche chiúin, oíche Mhic Dé,
Cách na suan, dís araon,
Dís is dílse faire le spéir,
Naíon beag gnaoigheal ceananntais caomh,
Críost 'na chodladh go séimh,
Críost 'na chodladh go séimh.

38

If you wish to include a more elaborate procession of light, Deirdre and Liam could return to light the candles held by E (emigrant) and Mo (Mother). Slowly, a line of lighted candles could then be formed by the eleven characters at the back of the stage as Deirdre and Liam walk front stage. Other options for this procession of light are included in the notes at the back of the script (Making Choices, pp. 41-45)

Spirit 1	I'm afraid our journey is almost over. Soon we'll be returning you back home again.
Deirdre	How can we ever thank you?
Spirit 3	I suppose some light refreshments would be out of the question?
Spirit 1	Yes they would! We can't have you gurgling your way forward to the twentieth century.
Liam	We'll never forget this amazing adventure, and of course now we can't EVER forget the real Spirit of Christmas.
Spirit 3	Looks like we've done a good job then! Now let's see, where is our next assignment?
Spirit 1	Bedrock, California.
Spirit 3	Yabadabadoo!
Liam:	Before you start pushing any of those buttons *(pointing to the computer)* we'd really like to make you a promise...
Spirit 2	A promise?
All candle-bearers	Yes! We'd like to promise that at Christmastime We'll STOP! And think of him, We'll give a little time to the one who matters most – Jesus, our Lord and our King.

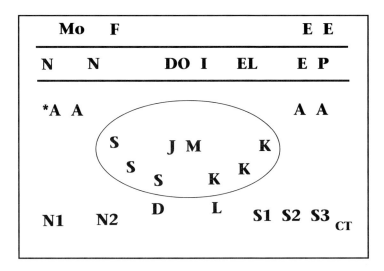

Deirdre and Liam shake hands with the spirits and there are some emotional hugs and goodbyes as all join in the finale.

SONG 8/FINALE   ***Mary's Boy Child***

Long time ago in Bethlehem, so the Holy Bible says,
Mary's boy child, Jesus Christ, was born on Christmas Day.

Chorus:

Hark now hear the angels sing, 'A new king born today',
And man will live for ever more because of Christmas Day.
Trumpets sound and angels sing, listen to what they say...
That man will live for ever more because of Christmas Day.

While shepherds watch their flocks by night,
They see a bright new shining star.
They hear a choir sing a song, the music seems to come from afar.
Now Joseph and his wife Mary come to Bethlehem that night.
They find no place to lay the child, not a single room in sight.

Chorus

By and by they find a little nook in a stable so forlorn.
And in a manger cold and dark Mary's little boy was born.

Chorus

Optional Ending: *If you want to end the drama in a quieter and more poignant manner, you can end it with the singing of 'Silent Night', leaving out the closing lines of the spirits above and the lively singing of 'Mary's Boy Child'. If you choose this optional ending, then lengthen the birthday wishes given to Jesus just before 'Silent Night' is sung so that the real message of Christmas shines through:*
> *Happy Birthday, Jesus!*
> *Let us promise each Christmas night to stop and think of him.*
> *Let's find a little space every day for Jesus, our Lord and our King.*

MAKING CHOICES

Large or small cast?

The play has been written for a cast of thirty actors. However, this cast can easily be increased or decreased to suit your particular needs. If you wish to reduce the cast, simply reduce the number of friends, neighbours, emigrants, narrators etc.

The cast could also be increased, if necessary, by adding more friends, neighbours, narrators etc, or by adding many more characters to the nativity play itself, e.g. Elizabeth's husband Zachariah, a large group of people heading off to the census in Bethlehem, the crowds in Bethlehem itself, customers in the inn, more angels and shepherds or more 'visitors' to the stable in the final tableau etc.

Note: The characters Deirdre and Liam have leading roles, so try to choose strong actors to play these parts, as they will carry the opening scenes. Spirit 1 also has a strong speaking part and Spirit 3 is a comical character, so keep this in mind when selecting your cast. The gender of any of the characters can be changed, if necessary, e.g. Deirdre and Liam can easily be changed to Deirdre and Niamh or Dan and Liam, as both are equally suitable for the parts in question!

Young or older age-groups?

This play can be used in a variety of ways. It can be performed by one class alone or many classes can be used to create a larger-than-life production. If you want to involve a range of age-groups in the production, some classes could narrate, some could act and others could form a 'choir', providing the necessary musical and vocal accompaniment. Another choice would be to have older children do all the vocal work while very young children simply mime the scenes, creating interesting tableaux throughout the narration.

Narrator or narrators?

Choose whatever form of narration suits your group best. The drama has been written as if only one class of children is involved, and to keep it simple, only two voices are used in the narration of the Christmas story, one child speaking as Narrator 1 and a second child speaking as Narrator 2. These narrators are dressed in biblical costume and represent Simeon and Anna. 'ALL' on stage respond as 'narrators' from time to time also.

It is possible, however, to change the narration completely, e.g. one actor could narrate everything or the spirits could take on the role of narration. Spirit 1 could be Narrator 1 and Spirits 2 and 3 could take on the role of Narrator 1. Or you could have groups of children involved in the narration, e.g. a group or class speaking the lines as Narrator 1 and another class speaking as Narrator 2. Much depends on the number of pupils taking part in the drama. There are numerous possibilities for you to consider.

Full cast for five scenes?

Option 1

If you look at the opening stage diagram, below, you will see that in the prescribed staging of *The Gift* all the characters involved in the nativity scenes are placed backstage. These characters are dressed in biblical costume, in stark contrast to the modern dress of the other 'secular' actors on stage, so it is best to keep them somewhat separate. The biblical characters are not directly involved in the drama until the start of Scene 3. From Scenes 3 to 5, all of the cast are on stage almost all of the time. But is it actually better to include the biblical characters on stage or to leave them off stage as Scene 1 begins? There are several pros and cons.

The opening chorus in *The Gift* is not sung by the main actors on stage and need not necessarily be sung by any children. ('Winter Wonderland' is played on tape or CD, creating an effective Christmas atmosphere as the main actors on stage communicate the opening scene through mime.) So in this particular opening scene you do not need a large group of children on stage as the curtain opens. The life and vigour necessary to captivate the audience will be achieved by the happy strains of 'Winter Wonderland' filling the hall, the positive impact of a colourful set and the interesting action of the main characters on stage.

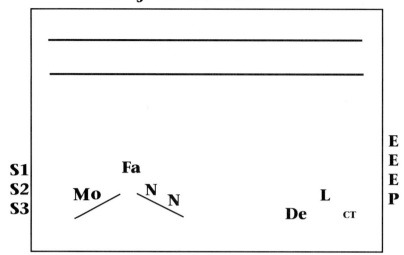

The advantage of keeping the biblical characters backstage, as shown above, is that these nativity characters would then pose no distraction for the audience later, and they could concentrate solely on the action taking place in the sitting-room. Otherwise their eyes might be drawn to the dazzling wings of angels or the rugged sheepskins of shepherds!

It could also be argued, on the other hand, that if out of sight, then out of mind also! There is, in fact, an ideal moment within the drama for the nativity characters to take their places on stage, namely as the instrumental 'Passage through Time' begins, at the end of Scene 2. As this music is being played, these actors could simply walk on stage and take their places at the back of the stage. However, let's now examine the possibility of keeping the biblical characters on stage throughout Scene 1 and Scene 2.

Option 2

Sometimes, depending on the particular children in question, it can prove more sensible to allow as many of the children as possible on stage from the start of the drama rather than keeping large numbers back or side stage. Firstly, this reduces the noise level backstage. Secondly, it means that almost all of the children can participate throughout the first scenes, even if only through gesture and song. Finally, meeting the whole cast as the curtain opens can have a very positive impact on an audience. Sometimes, if you leave children backstage it means that you have worries about control and supervision. Also, if the opening chorus is to be sung by the full cast the children back and side stage may be too excited to join in the singing and the opening chorus may seem lifeless and dead.

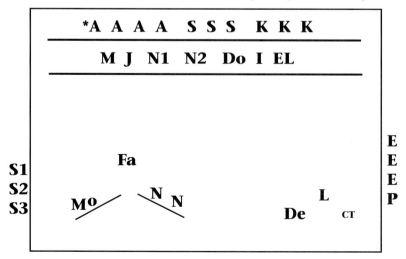

If you do decide to include the biblical characters on stage in Scene 1 it will be important to keep them somewhat separate from the secular sitting-room characters. So why not get the children to paint some simple scenic boards, a desert scene, perhaps, with rolling sands and thorny cacti or palm trees? By placing these scenic boards at either side of the biblical characters, but not directly in front of any of them, they then appear to be in a world of their own, separate from the actors in the sitting-room scene. More work, you say? If your own pupils are very busy preparing the play itself, perhaps another class could help with this art work. The more children involved in this project, the better.

Option 3

Another option you might consider, if the facility were available to you, would be to hide the biblical characters behind a separate curtain, at the back of the stage, as shown overleaf.

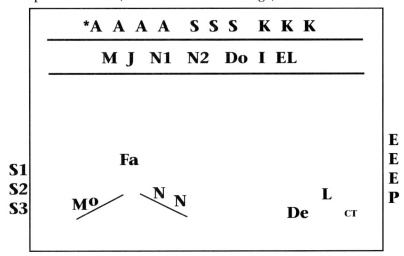

In choosing this staging you would have the best of both worlds. Your biblical characters would actually be in position on stage but they would also remain hidden, thereby proving no distraction to the scenes being enacted by the other children on stage.

Procession of light?

A candlelight procession has been included in the script of this drama, in Scene 5. In the closing scenes the main characters, Deirdre and Liam, come front stage, holding lighted candles, while a line of light is also formed by the characters at the back of the stage. These lights represent birthday candles as all the children wish the newborn infant a happy birthday, the light symbolising also the Light of the World having come among them. It is possible to exclude this scene if you so wish, but if you decide to include the procession of light, there are many possibilities for staging. The type of candlelight scene you choose largely depends on the number of children you wish to have involved in the drama.

The simplest option of all would be to use the main characters, Deirdre and Liam alone. They could proceed quite solemnly, front stage, holding their candles aloft as all on stage respond: 'Happy Birthday Jesus'. Or, alternatively, if you wish to increase the number in the cast you could use specific 'candleholders' who would participate in the drama at this stage.

If you want to involve a large number of children in the procession of light you could organise a junior or senior class, not involved on stage itself, to take on the role of candleholders, processing from the back of the hall or church, and taking their places on the hall floor in front of the stage, or even in the aisles of the hall where they could be seen by all. At the appropriate moment they raise their candles, as the cast respond, wishing Jesus a very happy birthday. Similarly, you could have a junior or senior class actually waiting in the wings and bring them on stage just for this scene alone. Whichever option you choose, make sure that all candles are blown out immediately after this scene, ensuring safety for all on stage and in the hall.

Choosing carols

The music in this drama includes an opening Christmas song, four instrumental pieces and seven carols:

'The Little Drummer Boy'   'Gloria in Excelsis Deo'
'Song for Mary'   'Silent Night'/'Oíche Ciúin'

43

'Little Donkey'   'Mary's Boy Child'
'Away in a Manger'

It is not wise to sing every verse of every carol as it lengthens the drama too much and can also be quite boring! So choose carols the children enjoy singing and vary the length, singing two verses of one, three of another or one verse of another etc. Also, don't feel that you have to stick rigidly to the carols named above. The children may have their own favourite carols or they may have special Christmas songs or carols learned over the years that they might like to include in their drama. It is possible to change any of the carols to include one of your own choice as most carols have a suitable theme and will fit in well. If you are not concerned about the length of the drama you might like to add an extra carol or two in the opening scene or after the final scene. Sometimes it is nice to involve the audience, or maybe other classes within the school, and end the whole concert with a 'singalong'. You could even have a 'karaoke' style conclusion to the night's festivities by displaying the words of some favourite carols on a large screen for all in the hall or church to read, to sing and to enjoy.

Complete drama or nativity scenes alone?

If you wish to confine the theatrical production to the nativity scenes alone, leaving out the secular sub-plot, Scenes 1-2 (Spirit of Christmas), then begin the drama with Instrumental 1, 'The Little Drummer Boy' at the end of Scene 2. Let the curtains open to an 'Eastern' set as the biblical characters process on stage, led by a Drummer Boy. An instrumental of this carol can be played on tape or by musicians on or off stage.

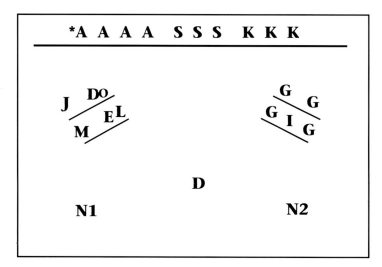

*The staging above is set for a cast of thirty, including the Innkeeper and his four guests (**G**) and perhaps a group of five children as **N1** and another group of five children as **N2**. But the number in the cast can be increased or decreased to suit your own needs.*

As the instrumental ends, the Drummer Boy marches front stage and announces:

Drummer Boy   *A poor young Drummer Boy am I*
With so few treasures but with great joy.
Please listen as my tale we tell,
A tale which makes my young heart swell.
For I now know the true wealth I've been given
By my Lord and God who lives in Heaven.
You too can share this wealth and joy
If you welcome into your heart a very special boy...

A verse or two of 'The Drummer Boy' is then sung as the play continues with the introductory lines of the narration: 'Mary was working at home one day...' The drama unfolds from here, through Scenes 2-5, ending with 'Silent Night' (see 'Optional Ending') and omitting any further lines from the spirits or from Deirdre or Liam.

44

HALL OR CHURCH?

The play can be staged in a school hall or in a church as part of the Christmas liturgical celebrations. Some churches are very suited to dramatic productions as they have large, open sanctuaries. But even where space is limited and where a pulpit may be blocking the view of the congregation, it is still possible to stage the nativity play effectively.

If staging this particular nativity play in a church, 'choral speakers' (i.e. narrators) could tell the story to the right and left of the main altar, standing on steps to give them height. As many or as few narrators as you wish could be used – two groups of four, two groups of ten or fifteen, two separate classes or just two narrators alone. Keep the space in front of the altar free for the nativity tableau itself.

Meanwhile, the actors could sit in suitable positions in the church, ready to mime the story at the appropriate time. Both the main aisle of the church and the space in front of the altar can be used in staging the drama. The aisle of the church is very suitable for enacting many of the nativity scenes, e.g. Mary walking towards Elizabeth, Mary and Joseph heading up and down the aisle towards Bethlehem, shepherds minding their flocks mid-aisle etc. The congregation may have to turn their heads to view some of the action, but this gives a real sense of involvement. A pulpit is ideal for hiding an angel who can pop up, at the appropriate time, during the Annunciation scene. As the drama progresses, the final tableau can be created in front of the altar, beside the choral speakers, in view for all. Of course, if you have a lot of space in the sanctuary it may be possible and more sensible to enact all of the drama there, in front of the main altar, and avoid the 'drama in the aisle' completely!

Church lighting can also be used effectively. Lights could be dimmed as Mary and Joseph head to the stable. Some lights at the back of the church could be turned back on as Mary and Joseph emerge with the tiny child in their arms and hold him up for all to see. As the couple and child walk towards the front of the altar and take their position for the final tableau the lighting could be increased. Candlelight could be used effectively by some visitors to the manger, to create a peaceful, spiritual atmosphere.

I have staged *The Gift* in my own church and have found the local community most appreciative and very moved by the children's performances. It proved a great way of sharing the children's work with the wider community as opposed to the school community alone. Also, Christmastime is one particular time of the year when adults seem to listen and to pay more attention to the wisdom of children. *The Gift* just might succeed in bringing the 'Good News' to life, helping adults to experience the joy and hope of Christ in their lives in a tangible and meaningful way at Christmastime.

PROPS

The sitting-room scene

Keep the stage as uncluttered as possible to allow free and easy movement for all. The opening set creates the 'sitting-room' scene. A small two-seater couch, two armchairs and a coffee table will provide the basic set. Some brightly coloured cushions scattered on the chairs and sofa would look well. Dress the coffee table with some teacups, a pot of tea, some Christmas cake and biscuits, etc. One other piece of furniture to display the music-centre, some photographs and perhaps a bunch of flowers, would be effective to set the scene. You could also hang lots of Christmas decorations around the room, if possible. Keep the Christmas tree as far to the right and to the front of the stage as you can so that it won't hinder the audience's view in any way.

The Eastern set

As the cast journey through time some stagehands can move the furniture off stage. Some large scenic boards could be placed at the back and to the sides of the stage to create 'the Eastern set' for the nativity play proper. Some cacti plants, tall cheese plants etc. could be placed to the front of the stage to create an 'Eastern look'. If it is too awkward to move the music-centre it could be covered with a colourful cloth and some earthenware jugs and mugs placed on top of it instead. Just train your stagehands to move smoothly and effectively.

A Christmas Tree in the Holy Land?

A Christmas tree (**CT**) is included in the stage diagrams at all times. It forms part of the sitting-room set and adds a real Christmas flavour to the staging. However, if it is a small artificial tree it could be removed at the end of Scene 2 as the children head to the Holy Land. I'm not sure how plentiful Norway Spruce were in Nazareth in the year of our Lord! But if it is too awkward to remove the tree at this time it can remain on stage throughout the play. Before the drama begins, place the tree as far to the side and out to the front of the stage as possible, perhaps even in front of the stage curtains. Then it will not interfere with the nativity scenes. If you are performing this nativity play as part of a school concert, the tree could be left on stage throughout the concert and perhaps add to the Christmas atmosphere and enhance the other dramas on stage.

Some general points

When choosing props, try not to choose ones that are inappropriate, e.g. props which are so small that they can't even be seen, or props which are so big that they can cause obstruction on stage. Also try not to use props which are completely unnecessary and a waste of valuable space. Keep the overall production as simple as possible. However, do remember that appropriate and interesting props can have a very positive visual impact on the audience and add greatly to the overall enjoyment of the drama.

Costumes

The biblical characters

Costumes suitable for use in a nativity play are not difficult to design, e.g. to simulate Eastern head-dress just wrap a colourful towel around the head and tie (tightly!) with a multi-coloured headband. Long tunics can be made by wrapping a large bright towel across the shoulder and tying it at the waist with a belt or cord. A plain-coloured T-shirt could be worn underneath the tunic for effect. Mary could wear a light blue shawl over a dark blue dress and Joseph could wear a combination of browns and creams in a tunic over leggings. The donkey in the play needs to be able to walk around – and sing! – so you could dress him in grey and give him a donkey mask to wear. If you have some sheepskin available to you it could be used to enhance the dress of the shepherds. Grannies might be able to provide 'staffs' for your shepherds. White sheets, tin-foil wings and tinsel haloes dress angels well. The kings need golden crowns, long glitzy robes (Dads' dressing gowns!) and coloured cloaks (tablecloths or rugs). One king should also carry a few large rolls of astrological maps. If you are setting up a mini 'inn scene', some wine caskets and earthenware jugs and mugs of different sizes would look well.

The secular characters

Bright, colourful costumes bring any drama to life so don't be conservative when choosing the wardrobe for your secular cast. These characters can be dressed as creatively as you like. Decide what type of character the Mother is, e.g. plump and homely or sophisticated and glamorous, and dress her to suit. Pay attention to smaller details, e.g. shoes, hairstyle, jewellery etc. Likewise with Father – specs, a pipe etc. can be used to enhance his character. Try to locate an authentic-looking cap and mailbag for the postman and some brightly wrapped Christmas gifts and cards for him to deliver to the household.

The costumes you choose for neighbours and emigrants can bring those characters to life also, e.g. if the emigrants are coming home from the US they might wear sneakers, Irish báinín sweaters, and peaked 'Ireland' caps. They could carry interesting-looking luggage bags covered in travel stickers. Costume can also be used to make the neighbours in the cast interesting. I often find that the children themselves are very creative when it comes to dresssing up. It's amazing what ideas they can have or what 'antiques' they can pull out of the attic. Also the casting of the characters is very important, e.g. the small child in the class, if given the correct part, can often bring a smile to the audience's faces. Likewise the heavy child or the extrovert. Some children have character no matter how they are dressed, so cast your drama carefully.

The Spirit of Christmas

The 'Spirits' in this drama could be dressed entirely in black, e.g. black leggings and T-shirts. Or you might prefer black leggings and red T-shirts or black leggings and a red, green and silver T-shirt, a different Christmas colour for each Spirit. You could decide to bring out the character of each spirit through costume, e.g. Spirit 1 'who is the serious and wise spirit leader' could wear a black suit, a white shirt and business tie. He could also wear small round specs and carry a briefcase. When taking the children on a journey through time he could use a lap-top computer of some sort, taken out of his briefcase for effect. Spirit 2 is the caring spirit with heart – his black T-shirt could be covered in red hearts. Spirit 3, the comical spirit, could wear zany black flares and multicoloured shirt. You can decide on the gender of the spirits yourself – all male, male/female etc.